THE BASICS OF MAKING HOMEMADE WINE AND VINEGAR

HOW TO MAKE AND BOTTLE WINE, MEAD, VINEGAR, AND FERMENTED HOT SAUCE

DAVID NASH

Copyright © 2019 by David Nash

All rights reserved.

No part of this book may be reproduced in any form or by any electronic or mechanical means, including information storage and retrieval systems, without written permission from the author, except for the use of brief quotations in a book review.

PREFACE

Since you are reading a book on self-reliance, I am assuming you want to know more about how to take care of yourself in disaster situations

I would like to suggest you take a moment and visit my website and YouTube channel for thousands of hours of free content related to basic preparedness concepts

Dave's Homestead Website
https://www.tngun.com

Dave's Homestead YouTube Channel
https://www.youtube.com/tngun

Shepherd Publishing
https://www.shepherdpublish.com

1

WHY MAKE HOMEMADE WINE

There are many reasons to make homemade wine, from health to being cost conscious, but for me it's the experience of doing something on my own and freeing myself from reliance on a store for something I enjoy.

This freedom soon translates into artistic license. Once you learn the technique and science behind wine making you are free to experiment. Then you can create wines from fruits and vegetables that you grow.

Making wine can become a hobby, or just a way to put food aside. Therefore, you can spend as much or as little time, effort, and resources as you desire. I personally enjoy a cold glass of sweet tea much more than a glass of chardonnay. However, I DO enjoy seeing others enjoy the products of my labor and skill. It is pleasing to me, and worth the effort to give a bottle of MY wine as a gift, or to enjoy it with someone.

Homemade Wine is Healthy

We all know about the French paradox. The French as a culture eat as much (or more) of the fatty foods as we do but have a much lower instance of heart disease than out American culture. While the entire reason for this is unclear. There is much evidence that the flavonoids found in the skins, seeds, stems, and pulp of dark grapes protect against heart attacks, blood clots, hardening of the arteries, Alzheimer's, and kidney stones. It has also been bound that fermenting grape juice allows more of the flavonoids to be released than pressing into juice alone.

Making Wine is a Good Disaster Prep

From a disaster prep standpoint, making wine has two good purposes. Utility of them can be decided upon by the reader. The first is barter. If you put aside a bottle or two from every batch of wine you make, over the course of a year you will have a decent store of wine, This collection could be traded for items you may not have. The second is that throughout history fermented beverages were served almost exclusively in place of water. This is because without modern infrastructure, it can become difficult to purify water. The fermentation process kills many harmful organisms. Additionally, the alcohol contained in wine serves as a good preservative.

HOW TO CHEAPLY MAKE HOMEMADE WINE

The recipe works whatever reason you want to try to make your own wine. Below is a simple beginner recipe that you can try before you decide to invest money in a better "quality" wine.

How to Make Homemade Wine Cheaply

Equipment:

- 5 gallon jug, carboy, or bucket with a tight fitting lid
- Airlock
- Funnel
- Rubber stopper
- Stockpot

Ingredients:

- 4 cans 100% grape juice concentrate, thawed (try to get a brand without sulfides. Sulfides are a preservative that inhibits fermentation)
- 4 pounds sugar

- 5 Gallons *unchlorinated* water (if using tap, its best to let it sit a couple days to let the chlorination dispel)
- Wine yeast

Procedure:

1. Clean the container with hot water. It is vital that your fermentation container is clean and sterile. You do not want your juice to rot you want it to ferment. So you must kill any bad bacteria. Remember, you cannot sterilize something until it is clean.
2. Pour the four cans of grape juice concentrate into the bucket. If using a carboy or jug, you will need the funnel.
3. Pour in enough water to make 3 1/2 gallons of grape juice/water mixture.
4. Measure 1/2 gallon of water into a large stockpot. Heat over low heat and add the 4 pounds of sugar. Stir until the sugar is completely dissolved. One this solution of sugar and water is completely dissolved add the entire pot of water to your fermentation container.
5. Measure 3 tablespoons of sugar into a small bowl. Add 1 package of wine yeast. Add 1/4 cup hot water. I have used bread yeast and champagne yeast also. The alcohol content may be slightly different. The fermentation times may change, but it will all work.
6. It should take about 10 minutes for the yeast to activate. Once it has become "bubbly" pour the yeast mixture into the jug.
7. Secure the airlock and rubber stopper on the carboy. Set the carboy in a spot where it will not be disturbed and the temperature doesn't have a lot of fluctuation.
8. Allow the wine mixture to ferment for approximately one month. When the airlock no longer bubbles when the jug or carboy is tapped, the wine is done.

Tips on Storing While Fermenting

During the fermenting stage I keep my wine in a bedroom closet. It is close enough where I can check it, the temperature is stable. Plus I don't have to see it if I chose not too.

I do make a concession to my bride. I keep the fermenting bucket in a big plastic container so in the event any sloshes out it will be collected and not stain her carpet.

HOW TO BOTTLE AND CORK HOMEMADE WINE

Bottling wine is an important part of wine making. First, ensure your wine is ready to be bottled. Meaning it is finished fermenting, clear, stable, and free of CO2. I do this by using a wine rack held in the fermentation vessel (5 gallon bucket) near the bottom, but not ON the bottom. I do not want to suck up all the dead yeast and other sediment.

Rack the Wine

After racking the wine into a clean vessel, I let it sit overnight to let any fines settle. I want to make sure that all the yeast is dead and that the sugar has been ate by the yeast. If there is any live yeast and sugar in the wine, then it will continue to ferment in the bottle, which would make my wine full of CO2, which is great if you want sparkling wine, but not so great if you don't. Stirring the wine is also a good idea, as that will release any suspended CO2.

Clean the Bottles

Next you want to make sure your bottles are clean and sanitary. This is very important, and common airborne bacteria eats alcohol and metabolizes acetic acid, like yeasts eat sugar and metabolize alcohol. If you do not clean your bottles well, then you may be surprised with a nice bottle of homemade vinegar.

Fill the Bottles

For the video I used a bottling wand to fill my bottles, it was very easy to use, and prevented a lot of waste. A bottling wand is a rigid tube with a pressure valve at the end. The wand fits on the end of the siphon tube to help you fill your bottles. When you insert the want in the bottom of the bottle and press, the valve opens and allows wine to flow. The bottle is then filled to the very rim of the bottle. When removed, the space taken by the wand allows the wine level inside the bottle to drop to just the right amount of headspace for the cork.

Cork and Let Settle

Depending on the type of cork and the type of corker, you may need to soak your corks for a duration ranging from a few minutes to overnight. This lubricates the corks so that they compress easily to make a good seal. The soaking water should have campden tablets, or other food safe disinfectant to ensure a sanitary process.

After you cork your wine, it is best to let the bottle sit upright for a couple of days to let any dissolved gasses release and work up past the cork. This allows for a better seal.

Once the wine has rested, then you can store your wine is a cool, dry, and dark place. It is best to store the wine on it's side so that the wine can keep the cork moist.

If you plan on keeping your wine for decades, you may want to consider recorking it every 5 or 6 years.

HOW TO CORK WINE USING A HANDI CORKER

I enjoy making my own wine, especially from fruits we have grown our self, when I started winemaking I just racked the wine into mason jars, but as I learned more about what was happening, I realized that mason jars could not handle the pressure created by secondary fermentation (like what happens when making champagne and sparkling wines, it also did not do justice to the work it takes to make a quality wine

So I began looking at my options. I can get wine bottles for decent prices. My local winemaking supply store sells bottles they have gotten from a local winery for around $16 a case. Corks are not that expensive either.

Corks Cost

- Natural corks are around $15 for 100 or $100 for 1000 corks.
- Synthetic corks for longer storage are a little more expensive and are around $20 for 100, or $185 for 1000.

With corks and bottles easy to find, and cheap enough so that I can slip them in the house without explaining the debit card transaction to *The Wife*. All I needed to do was to decide what to use to actually cork the wine.

Why I Got a Handi-Corker

I decided on a handi-corker to start with. I chose it primarily because it cost less than $10.00, and my research said it was pretty easy to use as long as I did not try to cork a lot of bottles at one time.

The instructions were printed on the side of the box and were very simple. Soak the corks overnight. That is it. The device is pretty intuitive, you simply stick the corker on the top of the bottle, shove a cork into it, and press firmly on the plunger until the cork is compressed into the bottle.

My friend (who is very serious about his alcohol production) told me I may want to have a rubber mallet, so I got one out, but I did not have to use it.

In my opinion, this device is worth the money, and is pretty easy to use. But if I was going to do more than a couple cases of wine I would invest in a better corker.

HOW TO MAKE A GALLON OF MEAD EASILY

This easy mead recipe is technically a melomel and not mead as I have fruit in the mead during primary fermentation. However, I generally don't make that fine of a distinction. It is based on honey from my bees and it is alcoholic. In contrast, traditional mead has only yeast, honey, and water.

Why make mead?

I don't drink much, but I love making stuff, and one of the reasons I got bees was that I was intrigued about how you could take a material with natural antibiotic properties (honey) and make something that required growth of "germs" (yeasts in alcohol).

I wanted to make mead. My local wine making mentor told me that he did not make a lot of mead because it was expensive (Using store bought honey), took a lot of time (he quoted a year), and it had a distinctive taste not everybody liked. He said if I really wanted to invest in mead making, I should go to the store and buy some wine to see if really liked it.

Apparently beer stores consider mead a fortified wine, and liquor stores consider it a beer, so it took me much wailing and gnashing of teeth until I could find someone to order me some. It was pretty good, and reinforced my desire to brew some.

I thought mead tasted good, so I started researching and looking for an easy mead recipe.

Things to know before making mead

If you're going to make mead, here are some things to think about:

Pure honey does not have enough moisture to keep bacteria alive. It won't ferment until it is mixed with water.

Honey does not contain a lot of the nutrients yeasts need to grow rapidly. So, while the inverted sugars are great for making alcohol, you will need to add nutrients to speed the fermentation process.

Time is an ally, while this recipe will be technically ready at about 2 months, the flavors won't develop into something "good" for 8 months to a year.

Basic 1 Gallon Recipe for a Basic Melomel Mead

Ingredients:

- 1 gallon spring water
- 2 to 3 lbs of unprocessed honey (2 makes a dry wine while 3 makes a sweeter wine)
- 1 package of active dry yeast (you can get away with bread yeast. I used a package of lavin, which is a brewing yeast. I know some that use a champagne yeast.)
- Small box of raisins (20 or so)
- An orange divided into eights
- Gallon glass jar (I got mine from a restaurant supply store, if previously it held apple cider)
- Bung (I used a rubber 8 ½ bung which fit my jug)

- Airlock (though if you're really cheap you could use a balloon with a small hole. However, a bung and airlock are only $2.00 and they work much better and lasts infinitely longer)

Procedure:

- Make sure everything is clean and sterile. While you can use natural yeasts (ever had sweet tea ferment on you?) You are rolling the dice and can end up with nasty mold and gunk instead of clean alcohol.
- Gently heat your honey in a double boiler, or in a pot of hot water. The warmer it is, the easier it will flow.
- Empty half of the water out of the 1 gallon jug into a large bowl or pitcher. The honey takes up a lot of space. Don't pout the water out though, because you might need some of it to top the jug off.
- Pour in the honey. Make sure not to waste it and get it on the sides of the jug. Honey is sticky and expensive.
- Add the yeast
- Add 15 to 20 raisins and screw the cap pack on the jug.
- Drop in the oranges (optional)
- Vigorously shake the jug for several minutes to thoroughly mix and aerate the mix.
- Remove the cap and add just enough spring water to leave an inch or two of head space.
- Stick the airlock in the hole in your rubber bung
- Fill the airlock halfway with water (vodka, or pure grain neutral spirit works better, if you can stand to "waste" it).
- Install the rubber bung with airlock in the top of the jug
- Set the jug of must in a cool dark space and wait…

Additional mead-making information

Within 24 hours fermentation should begin and you will see bubbles climbing up the sides of the jug.

After 7 to 10 days of fermentation (depending on temperature warmer is faster, too hot kills the yeast, too cold the yeast go to sleep), you should no longer see bubbles.

If you see bubbles rising wait a few more days to ensure fermentation has completed.

Next, the mead should be racked (transferred) into a different sanitary container (jug, bottle, etc) taking care to leave behind the sediment and raisins.

Finally, an additional 6 to 10 months storage in a cool dark place will result in a tasty mead from this easy mead recipe.

6

HOW TO MAKE HARD APPLE CIDER THE EASY WAY

As with all my home "brew" recipes this one for Hard Apple Cider is a very basic recipe. Serious aficionados will have much more sophisticated ways of going about it. Using named yeast strains instead of bread yeasts will give you a much better product with a repeatable taste.

Typically, Americans consider cider to be unfiltered apple juice. Consequently, hard cider is alcoholic. Most everywhere else, cider is fermented apple juice.

Today we will be making hard cider from store-bought ingredients.

Ingredients:

- One gallon of cider. Organic is preferred as preservatives will interfere with the fermentation process
- One can of 100% apple juice concentrate, once again try to find one without sulfates.
- Yeast. Available at any brewing store. Look for a wine or champagne strand. I used a Lavin (the number escapes me).

You can use bread yeast but you may not get the same quality of final product.

Materials:

- Large pot, two gallon minimum
- Candy thermometer
- Plastic spoon
- Sanitizer (Unscented bleach will work for now)
- Rubber stopper and airlock to fit the gallon jug (Available at any brewing store)

Directions:

- Sanitize all your equipment. This is the most important step. Bacterias and mold can kill your project quickly. Sanitize by mixing a ratio of one tablespoon of bleach per one gallon of water. Submerge your equipment, in a clean sink or bathtub. Let the materials sit for 20 minutes and rinse thoroughly.
- Heat up one gallon of organic apple juice on the stove. You want to keep it just below boiling for a few minutes. This is known as pasteurization and kills off any contaminants without burning off the sugars that flavor the cider and provide food for the yeast.
- Next, cover the cider and allow to cool. While it is cooling, follow the directions on whichever yeast you have selected to reconstitute it. When the juice has cooled to the temperature listed on the yeast packet, pitch in the yeast, cap the bottle and shake vigorously to introduce air into the mixture.
- Lastly, cap the bottle with the stopper and airlock. Make sure to fill the airlock with either water or vodka so carbon dioxide can be released without allowing contaminants in.
- Wait about six weeks. You will see bubbles in about 24 hours coming from the airlock.
- After six weeks, Siphon off the cider into a pot and clean out

the inside of the jug. The slurry at the bottom of the jug is dead yeast and other materials that have settled.

- Taste the cider, if it tastes good to you, rebottle it and put it into your fridge. If it is too dry, try sweetening it with the apple juice concentrate. Heat up the cider on the stove and add the concentrate until the desired flavor is achieved. If you have not added wine-making chemicals (such as sulfates) to kill the yeast, you must keep this cold, otherwise, the yeast will eat the sugar and produce CO2, which can cause your bottle to explode.
- Finally, the cider is ready to drink at this point. If you are patient, the flavor will improve over time and the cider will start to become clearer in the fridge.

7

HOW TO MAKE, TEST, FEED, AND STORE HOMEMADE VINEGAR

Making my own homemade vinegar was something I have been interested in for some time; however, I thought it was difficult. Turns out I was wrong.

Making vinegar is just a simple (if not more so) than making wine. Just as yeast eat sugar and excrete alcohol. Acectobacter eats alcohol and excretes acetic acid (vinegar). They both need a warm dark place to do their work. However, yeast works in an anaerobic environment, vinegar is formed in an aerobic environment. So keep your alcohol away from air, or it may turn to vinegar.

All you really need is a warm dark place, a jug, an alcoholic beverage, cheesecloth or other means of keeping out debris while allowing airflow, and a mother (a starter culture of acetobacter). Fortified wines, ports, and liquors don't work as well as the wine and beers that are around 6% alcohol.

You can order a mother from several places online for 16 to 20 dollars, and generally they will be listed as either a red, white, or malt mother. The Acectobacter is the same culture, it is just in a different liquid so you don't make a pretty white wine discolored by adding a couple cups of red wine to it.

Cheaper Alternative to Buying a Culture

Now, if you think about it, and realize what you are doing by buying a mother, you could probably find a mother culture somewhere else. I noticed that the apple cider vinegar my wife buys is labeled "raw and unpasteurized". Reading further I noticed at the bottom of the label it said: "with mother" … a furry of internet queries later I saw that several people have made vinegar using the mother from *"Bragg's Raw Apple Cider Vinegar"*.

How to Make Homemade Vinegar

- Dump any leftover wine or beer (not both) into a crock, jug, or other stainless steel, ceramic, or glass container. (Aluminum, cast iron, or plastic containers will not work)
- Dilute with a little water, no more than 50/50, and you want to leave room in the container for air to get in. The more surface area the faster your mother will grow. Also don't use tap water unless you give it time for the chlorine to evaporate (it will kill your mother).
- Dump in the mother. I made sure to get some of the chunks from the bottom of the Bragg's jar, but I don't think it is necessary. About one cup per gallon should work.
- Cap with a piece of cheesecloth held in place with a rubber band.
- Shake a little (again probably not necessary)
- Store in a dark closet and come back in about 2 months.

Additional Tips

You should have a leathery growth floating at the top of the liquid. A floating culture is a healthy mother. If you don't then you may need to feed your vinegar with some fresh wine and a teaspoon or so of more raw vinegar.

If you have a vinegar crock with a tap near the bottom, you can use it by tapping it as needed. After you take some out top it off with whatever wine you have around as you open a bottle and don't finish all off it.

How to Test, Feed, and Store Homemade Vinegar

Now that the vinegar has had time to steep, it's time to see about using it.

Before I am able to can with my vinegar I have to get set up for testing homemade vinegar.

First off, when I brought the jar up from the basement it smelled very stout, However, smelling is pretty subjective. If you are going to use your vinegar for food preservation it must contain at least 5% acid.

Typically vinegar contains 5-20% by volume with 5% being the most common in the grocery store.

This is different from pH, but fI used pH strips from the brew shop to see just how strong my vinegar was as it needed to have a pH lower than 4.6 to be able to be considered "high acid" as it relates to canning.

High and Low Acid Food

The Difference between pressure canning and boiling water canning is high or low acid foods. This cut off is a pH of 4.6 anything less than a pH of 4.6 is considered a high acid food.

I have read that botulism cannot reproduce at a pH of 4.4 or less. The food you can, as well as the moisture from it will change the pH by diluting your pickling solution.

I do not consider my vinegar to be vinegar until it reaches at least a pH of 5, However, I wait until it is at least a 4 on the scale before I use it for canning (but I will make refrigerator pickles with a pH of 5)…

Testing Vinegar

To test, I just poured out a sample, stuck my test strips in the liquid, and then compared it to the picture on the jar. The set of strips was a reasonable cost. They were around $7 for a jar full of strips.

However, you need to know that the FDA doesn't allow commercial canneries to use pH paper to test. There are two reasons for this:

- Comparing colors is relatively subjective
- Accuracy of the strips can degrade over time.

Storing Vinegar

Some of my vinegar made the cut. So I stored it in a jugs. While you can buy clean empty milk jugs, the vinegar will eat through it. Use glass jars for storage. Many folks that make their own vinegar have one continuously fed batch. As they use it, they refill it. That is basically what I do. As I use mine, I just top it off with whatever leftover wine I have around.

Feed Regularly

In a perfect world, you should feed your vinegar regularly. It needs the alcohol from the wine to keep the culture strong. If you don't feed it regularly, the mother may collapse and sink to the bottom. This is because it will go dormant if it eats all the alcohol.

Making vinegar isn't really all that hard, and it is so much more fulfilling to cook with vinegar I made from wine I fermented from fruits I grew…. It may just be me, but mustard made from my home-made vinegar is so much tastier than store bought…

8

60 USES FOR VINEGAR

1. Arthritis tonic and treatment; 2 spoonfuls of apple cider vinegar and honey in a glass of water several times daily.

2. Thirst-quenching drink: apple cider vinegar mixed with cold water.

3. Sagging cane chairs: sponge them with a hot solution of half vinegar and half water. Place the chairs out in the hot sun to dry.

4. Skin burns: apply ice cold vinegar right away for fast relief. Will prevent burn blisters.

5. Add a spoonful of vinegar to cooking water to make cauliflower white and clean.

6. Storing cheese: keep it fresh longer by wrapping it in a vinegar-soaked cloth and keeping it in a sealed container.

7. Remove stains from stainless steel and chrome with a vinegar-dampened cloth.

8. Rinse glasses and dishes in water and vinegar to remove spots and film.

9. Prevent grease build-up in your oven by frequently wiping it with vinegar.

10. Wipe jars of preserves and canned food with vinegar to prevent mold- producing bacteria.

11. To eliminate mildew, dust and odors, wipe down walls with vinegar-soaked cloth.

12. Clean windows with vinegar and water.

13. Hardened paint brushes: simmer in boiling vinegar and wash in hot soapy water.

14. Clean breadbox and food containers with vinegar-dampened cloth to keep fresh-smelling and clean.

15. Pour boiling vinegar down drains to unclog and clean them. 16. Clean fireplace bricks with undiluted vinegar.

17. An excellent all-purpose cleaner: vinegar mixed with salt. Cleans copper, bronze, brass, dishes, pots, pans, skillets, glasses, windows. Rinse well.

18. Make your catsup and other condiments last long by adding vinegar.

19. To clear up respiratory congestion, inhale a vapor mist from steaming pot containing water and several spoonfuls of vinegar.

20. Apple cider vinegar and honey as a cure-all: use to prevent apathy, obesity, hay fever, asthma, rashes, food poisoning, heartburn, sore throat, bad eyesight, dandruff, brittle nails and bad breath.

21. When boiling eggs, add some vinegar to the water to prevent white from leaking out of a cracked egg.

22. When poaching eggs, add a teaspoon of vinegar to the water to prevent separation.

23. Weight loss: vinegar helps prevent fat from accumulating in the body.

24. Canned fish and shrimp: to give it a freshly caught taste, soak in a mixture of sherry and 2 tablespoons of vinegar.

25. Add a spoonful of vinegar when cooking fruit to improve the flavor.

26. Soak fish in vinegar and water before cooking for a tender, sweeter taste.

27. Add vinegar to boiling ham to improve flavor and cut salty taste.

28. Improve the flavor of desserts by adding a touch of vinegar.

29. Add vinegar to your deep fryer to eliminate a greasy taste.

30. Add a tablespoon of vinegar to fruit gelatin to hold it firm.

31. Steep your favorite herb in vinegar until you have a pleasing taste and aroma.

32. Use vinegar instead of lemon on fried and broiled foods.

33. To remove lime coating on your tea kettle; add vinegar to the water and let stand overnight.

34. To make a good liniment: beat 1 whole egg, add 1 cup vinegar and 1 cup turpentine. Blend.

35. Apply vinegar to chapped, cracked skin for quick healing.

36. Vinegar promotes skin health: rub on tired, sore or swollen areas.

37. Reduce mineral deposits in pipes, radiators, kettles and tanks by adding vinegar into the system.

38. Rub vinegar on the cut end of uncooked ham to prevent mold. 39. Clean jars with vinegar and water to remove odor.

40. Avoid cabbage odor by adding vinegar to the cooking water. 41. Skunk odor: remove from pets by rubbing fur with vinegar.

42. Paint adheres better to galvanized metal that has been wiped with vinegar.

43. Pets' drinking water: add vinegar to eliminate odor and encourage shiny fur.

44. For fluffy meringue: beat 3 egg whites with a teaspoon of vinegar.

45. Pie crust: add 1 tablespoon vinegar to your pastry recipe for an exceptional crust.

46. Half a teaspoon per quart of patching plaster allows you more time to work the plaster before it hardens.

47. Prevent discoloration of peeled potatoes by adding a few drops of vinegar to water. They will keep fresh for days in fridge.

48. Poultry water: add vinegar to increase egg production and to produce tender meat.

49. Preserve peppers: put freshly picked peppers in a sterilized jar and finish filling with boiling vinegar.

50. Olives and pimentos will keep indefinitely if covered with vinegar and refrigerated.

51. Add 1 tsp. vinegar to cooking water for fluffier rice.

52. Add vinegar to laundry rinse water: removes all soap and prevents yellowing.

53. After shampoo hair rinse: 1 ounce apple cider vinegar in 1 quart of distilled water.

54. For a shiny crust on homemade bread and rolls: just before they have finished baking, take them out, brush crusts with vinegar, return to oven to finish baking.

55. Homemade sour cream: blend together 1 cup cottage cheese, 1/4 cup skim milk and 1 tsp. vinegar.

56. Boil vinegar and water in pots to remove stains. 57. Remove berry stains from hands with vinegar.

58. Prevent sugaring by mixing a drop of vinegar in the cake icing. 59. Cold vinegar relieves sunburn.

60. When boiling meat, add a spoonful of vinegar to the water to make it more tender.

61. Marinate tough meat in vinegar overnight to tenderize.

62. A strength tonic: combine raw eggs, vinegar and black pepper. Blend well.

63. Douche: 2 to 4 ounces of vinegar in 2 quarts of warm water.

9

RECIPE CHICKEN WITH VINEGAR

Cooking meat in vinegar is called cooking meat "Adobo". It is a cultural cooking process from the Philippines, where meat is marinated in vinegar, browned, and then simmered in the marinade. This process is worthwhile for preppers, homesteaders, or outdoorsmen to know because leftovers keep well without refrigeration because the vinegar inhibits bacteria.

In my experience it softens up tough meat, and I especially like using this process with rabbit. As a matter of fact, I make "chicken with vinegar" far more often with rabbit more than I do with chicken.

Cooking mellows the vinegar, as well as tenderizes the meat. The end result will be about as tart as cooking chicken with tomatoes. It is actually pretty good, and I end up keeping a jug of my homemade wine vinegar near my stove so I can throw in a cup or two into my cooking whenever the wife is not looking ...

Ingredients

- 2 tablespoons olive oil
- 1 3-pound cubed chicken

- Salt and freshly ground black pepper
- 1/4 cup minced shallots or scallions
- 1 cup good red-wine vinegar
- 1 tablespoon butter (optional)

Procedure

1. Preheat the oven to 450 degrees.
2. Set a large ovenproof skillet over medium-high heat. .
3. Add oil
4. When it is hot, place chicken in the skillet, skin side down.
5. Cook undisturbed for about 5 minutes, or until chicken is nicely browned.
6. Turn and cook 3 minutes on the other side. Season with salt and pepper.

HOW TO TURN A MASON JAR INTO A FERMENTING CROCK USING A RECAP LID

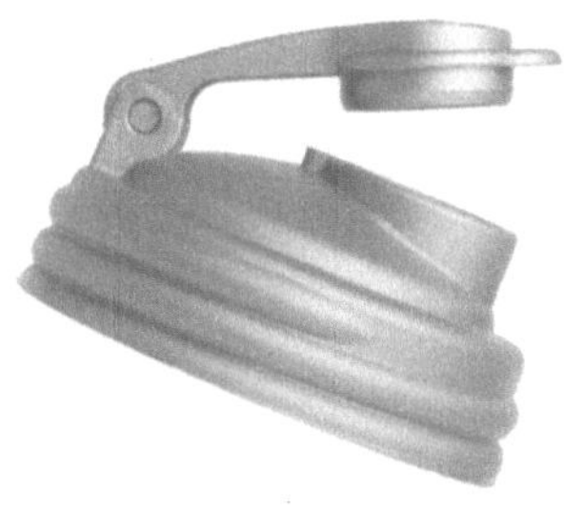

I have a link to the cap mentioned on my website. https://www.tngun.com/mason-jar-recap-lid-for-fermenting/

If you want to ferment a small batch of something, probably not wine, but for something like kefir, kombucha, vinegar, or a fermented pepper mash, a gallon jug is overkill, plus with larger fermented foods, getting the product out of a large carboy is difficult. In this case, you may want to ferment in a mason jar. It would work great for those foods mentioned.

The problem is that they don't make bungs big enough to stopper a mason jar. What you can do is to get a screw on lid with a flip top (generally used to make a drinking glass from the jar) and then use a rubber 6 ½ bung and a two piece airlock it becomes a handy fermenter for small batches of stuff.

I think this is a pretty cool little tip, and while I don't use it often, it is my go to for when I make a fermented pepper mash for hot sauce.

11

HOW TO MAKE HOT PEPPER MASH

When I was younger I could not tolerate hot food, but as I age, I find myself enjoying spicy food.

Couple that with my DIY gene, I really enjoy making my own hot sauce; it is not hard and makes a quality sauce for little expense.

This recipe works with any hot pepper, and I usually use a blend of jalapeño and habanero.

Making a pepper mash is different from making hot sauce. The sauce comes from the mash.

The pepper mash is fermented to mellow the flavor of the peppers and really adds to the quality. Tabasco sauce, for instance, is fermented for three years, but I find after 6 months you really don't get that much more quality.

Since we are letting the peppers ferment, we are going to be adding salt to suppress bad bacteria and mold.

What You Need

The first thing you are going to need is a glass jar or pottery crock, size matters as you only can fill it about ¾ full so it won't overflow as it ferments. You want a straight sided container so you can use a weighted plate to keep the peppers under the liquid (this prevents mold).

As you size your jug, realize that 1 pound of peppers will produce a little less than a pint of pepper mash.

As you pick your peppers, get the largest, plumpest fully ripe peppers from the garden or market. Fully ripe peppers have a higher sugar content, so that will help with fermentation.

I remove the seeds from my peppers, but that is a personal choice. Contrary to popular opinion, the seeds don't add much heat. The real heat comes from the connecting veins that attach the seeds to the pepper walls.

How to Make the Pepper Mash

- Wash the peppers and dry them with a towel or paper towel before processing them.
- Remove and discard the stems.
- Add 1 Tablespoon of salt per pint of mash
- Process the peppers in a blender.
- Pour one Tablespoon sea salt per pound of peppers in a blender and process them on high speed till they become puree (mash), no more than a minute at the absolute most, typically only 15 to 30 seconds
- You may add other vegetables, herbs, and spices into the blender and puree it along with the peppers mash, so long as you maintain the salt ratio to weight of vegetable matter.

Anything you add will dramatically affect the taste of the finished product, (I add sweet peppers)

- Pour the mash into the fermentation jar or crock. You need to keep air away from the mash, but if you seal it airtight it will explode. If you are using a straight sided crock, set an upside down plate inside the crock so that it can move up and down the crock, weigh it down with a ziplock bag full of water. Since I use a large juice carafe, I simply stick in a large rubber bung fitted with a airlock for making wine.

In one week, the pepper mash will start bubbling vigorously as a result of fermentation in which the bacteria will produce acetic acid and any sugars will produce alcohol and carbon dioxide gas. The gas bubbles will cause the pulp in the mash to rise, leaving the liquid and some solids on the bottom.

In another week or two, the fermentation should stop producing bubbles.

You may use the mash as soon as fermentation has finished. I let it age in a dark closet for about 6 months though.

You can use this mash directly on food. However it's a simple process to turn it into a sauce.

Turning Mash to Sauce

There are two ideas on how to turn your fermented pepper mash to sauce.

Basically Louisiana Hot Sauce is the strained liquid from your mash with maybe a little vinegar added. This is thin and free of seeds and such.

I like mine to be a little chunkier, so I tend to dump out the mash into a blender or food mill and puree it until it is smooth. You need to really chop up the mix or it will tend to separate into layers.

Bottling

After the fermentation process is finished, Typically the pH of the sauce is below 4.6 so you can boil it, funnel it into jars, and process it in a boiling water bath canner for 15 minutes. This treatment will kill off the bacteria in the sauce so that you don't have to refrigerate it.

BUNG SIZES FOR BREWING

I made this reference of what the numbers on the sides of the rubber stoppers mean in relation to size because I got tired of lugging whatever bottle I found into the brew store and tried on all then bungs for fit. I also heard myself on a video say my bung was too loose and never want to say that again ever.

Tips:

- #00 Stopper fits and plugs the airlock hole in a drilled stopper so it can be used as a solid stopper
- #2 Stopper fits standard wine bottle opening
- #6 Stopper fits wine making and beer brewing industry ½ and 1 gallon jugs
- #6.5 Stopper fits standard 6 gallon glass carboys
- #7 Stopper fits standard 3, 5, and 6.5 gallon glass carboys
- #10 Stopper fits standard 3, 5, and 6 gallon plastic carboys
- #11 Stopper fits Demi Johns (14.25 Gallon Glass Carboys)
- #11.5 Stopper fits most oak barrels

Stopper Size	Bottom Diameter (Inches)	Top Diameter (Inches)	Avg. Diameter (Inches)
#2	5/8	3/4	11/16
#3	11/16	7/8	13/16
#5.5	15/16	1-1/16	1
#6	7/8	1-1/4	1-1/8
#6.5	1	1-1/2	1-1/4
#7	1-3/16	1-7/16	1-5/16
#7.5	1-1/4	1-1/2	1-3/8
#8	1-5/16	1-9/16	1-7/16
#8.5	1-7/16	1-11/16	1-9/16
#9.5	1-1/2	1-3/4	1-5/8
#10	1-11/16	1-15/16	1-13/16
#10.5	1-13/16	2-1/16	1-15/16
#11	1-15/16	2-3/16	2-1/16
#11.5	2	2-1/2	2-1/4

PLEASE REVIEW

Please visit my Amazon Author Page at:

https://amazon.com/author/davidnash

if you like my work, you can really help me by publishing a review on Amazon.

The link to review this work at Amazon is:

https://www.amazon.com/review/create-review?asin=B07YGBMWS5

LINKS TO VIDEOS

The Basics of Homemade Cleaning Supplies: Playlist

http://yt.vu/p/PLZH3jGjLQ0rB2127yMtVAyr062nmbjws2

How to Make Homemade Wine Cheaply Part I

https://youtu.be/aaC8cBPLdIg

How to Make Homemade Wine Cheaply Part II

https://youtu.be/YSD7Eel5Af4

How to Bottle and Cork Homemade Wine

https://youtu.be/VbV12Q62N-4

How to Cork Wine Using a Handi-Corker

https://youtu.be/nU0EgmVDckY

How to Make a Gallon of Mead Easily (Melomel)

https://youtu.be/ToihuvUEbVM

How to Make Hard Apple Cider The Easy Way

https://youtu.be/3iW-lWLPShE

How to Make Homemade Vinegar

https://youtu.be/4REhkhH3Doo

How to Test, Feed, and Store Homemade Vinegar

https://youtu.be/Qq-AOzgT6J8

How to Turn A Mason Jar Into A Fermenting Crock Using a reCap Lid

https://youtu.be/ivZeYobu48o

The Basics of
Homemade Cleaning
Supplies
Homestead Basics Book 6
David Nash

What is the Difference Between Baking and Washing Soda

I am not a chemist, but I am a hazmat technician, so work made me take a fair amount of chemistry courses.

I have decided that I want to try my hand at making soap. It is easy DIY chemistry. Additionally, it is about the only chemistry left for the layman to "relearn" from our forefathers.

That being said, I keep finding recipes using washing soda, with a stern warning about not mixing it up with baking soda. Since I believe that most warning labels are posted in response to an act, I figure that people may get confused. So here is the difference:

Washing Soda vs Baking Soda

Washing soda is sodium carbonate: two sodium atoms, a carbon atom, and three hydrogen atoms.

Baking soda is sodium bicarbonate: the same ingredients, but with a hydrogen atom replacing one of the sodium.

What that means to us is that their pH is different. Baking soda is about an 8 on the scale (7 being neutral). Most of our body fluids (Stomach acid and urine are acids) are around a 7.4 Baking soda is not damaging to us.

Washing soda on the other hand is about an 11 on the scale so it is a lot higher on the scale. As a matter of fact, it is just corrosive enough to not be allowed to be labeled "non-toxic". You do not want to get this in your body.

But since washing soda is higher on the scale, it is can neutralize more acid, so its perfect for washing things like dirty diapers.

Now that you no the difference, turn the page and I will show you how to convert Baking Soda into Washing Soda.

If you like this Introduction to The Basics of Homemade Cleaning Supplies, you can find it on Amazon.

ALSO BY DAVID NASH

Homestead Basics

The Basics of Raising Backyard Chickens

The Basics of Raising Backyard Rabbits

The Basics of Beginning Beekeeping

The Basics of Homemade Cheesemaking

The Basics of Making Homemade Wine and Vinegar

The Basics of Homemade Cleaning Supplies

The Basics of Baking

The Basics of Food Preservation

The Basics of Food Storage

The Basics of Cooking Meat

The Basics of Make Ahead Mixes

The Basics of Beginning Leatherwork

Non Fiction

21 Days to Basic Preparedness

52 Prepper Projects

52 Prepper Projects for Parents and Kids

52 Unique Techniques for Stocking Food for Preppers

Basic Survival: A Beginner's Guide

Building a Get Home Bag

Handguns for Self Defense

How I Built a Ferrocement "Boulder Bunker"

New Instructor Survival Guide

The Prepper's Guide to Foraging

The Prepper's Guide to Foraging: Revised 2nd Edition

The Ultimate Guide to Pepper Spray

Understanding the Use of Handguns for Self Defense

Fiction

The Deserter: Legion Chronicles Book 1

The Revolution: Legion Chronicles Book 2

Note and Record Books

Correction Officer's Notebook

Get Healthy Notebook

Rabbitry Records

Collections and Box Sets

Preparedness Collection

Translations

La Guía Definitiva Para El Spray De Pimienta

Multimedia

Alternative Energy

Firearm Manuals

Military Manuals 2 Disk Set

ABOUT THE AUTHOR

David Nash is a suburban homesteader with chickens, bees, rabbits, and a couple of goats in his suburban yard. For a while he even had an extensive aquaponics setup in his basement, until his long-suffering wife made him eat all the fish.

He knows how to raise animals humanely, simply, and without angering the neighbors. Dave runs a popular YouTube channel on DIY homesteading as well as being the author of several books on DIY preparedness and urban homesteading topics.

In fact, the tips shown in this book contributed to him receiving the third highest preparedness score on the TV show Doomsday Preppers

He is a father and a husband. He enjoys time with his young son William Tell and his school teacher wife Genny. When not working, writing, creating content for YouTube, playing on his self-reliance blog, or smoking award-winning BBQ he is asleep.

amazon.com/author/davidnash

facebook.com/booksbynash

youtube.com//tngun

goodreads.com/david_allen_nash

twitter.com/dnash1974

instagram.com/shepherdschool

pinterest.com/tngun

www.ingramcontent.com/pod-product-compliance
Lightning Source LLC
Chambersburg PA
CBHW030410160726
47992CB00007B/3053